CN01656092

Converting your print book to ePUB & Kindle versions

Using InDesign CS5.5 & CS6

F2
F3
F4
Converting your print book to ePUB & Kindle versions
Using InDesign CS5.5 & CS6
Z
X
C
David Bergsland
alt
Radiqx PRESS
option
command

Written and published in June, 2012

ISBN-13: 978-1477687659
ISBN-10: 1477687653

Radiqx PRESS

Mankato, Minnesota • http://radiqx.com • info@radiqx.com

Please let us know if there is anyway I can help you in your publishing endeavors.

This is dedicated to my friends and readers who help keep me on track with their comments and reviews. I wouldn't get better at my craft nearly as quickly without the ones the Lord sends along side to help me. I'm grateful!

Contents

This booklet is slightly rewritten and updated from Appendix E in *Writing In InDesign Second Edition*

It is assumed that you have either read this book or that you know InDesign well enough so that you have everything formatted with styles. If you do not, these conversions will be very laborious.

ePUB Design from InDesign CS6

At this point I am assuming that you have a finished, formatted and uploaded book for print and probably a downloadable PDF. The question is how do we take this and convert it to an ePUB and a Kindle book?

If this is the case, everything in the book is formatted with styles, it is all edited and proofed, the copy is ready to go. If this is the case, then the conversion to ePUB and Kindle can go really fast.

Designing & formatting your ePUB & Kindle book without coding

Coding is anathema: Again, I must assume some things. My experience is that people like us can handle a little simple Web coding like XHTML and CSS (actually, most of us have been forced into it for our Websites). However, most people who do what we do really dislike coding.

Important announcement!
This booklet is current as of June 2012

This field of design is changing so rapidly that anything a month old is at least a bit out of date. The good news is that the methods I will cover here will still work. The bad news is that some of them may no longer be necessary. Earlier this year, we were dealing with image size issues for the Retina display of the new iPad, for example. I found new information about dealing with lists in April and had to test it before I could write that portion of this chapter. This week the largest problem is that we are still waiting for the new Amazon Kindle Export plug-in for CS6.

Fancy ePUBs require fancy coding

At this point in the development of ePUBs, ePUB design is commonly produced by coding specialists—especially for larger traditional publishers. Even though InDesign can export good validated ePUBs, a lot is still missing. It's not just missing from InDesign but from all WYSIWYG applications. This is because of one simple issue. In order to do simple things like text wraps (CSS: alignments), sidebars (CSS: divs), and all the rest, you must be able to crack the compressed ePUB file and mess with its innards (many files and folders).

I've written briefly about this in other places, but CS6 has made major strides to solve the text wrap and sidebar issues. However, it is still not clean and simple. Plus, there are many purely design issues which suggest that text wraps and sidebars do not work well in ebooks, regardless. More about that in a bit.

There is no simple program that allows you to do this visually. Dreamweaver is the obvious candidate for this capability, but nothing has been done yet by Dreamweaver. As a result, all of these things must be done on the code level and most of us are simply not ready to do that. It is possible to do the editing in Dreamweaver, but it is not pleasant and it is certainly not a good design experience. You need to make some tough decisions about your ebooks.

InDesign CS5.5 can produce validated ePUBs: but you must rethink your book layouts severely.

InDesign CS6 has done quite a bit to write better code: but it still takes a lot of setup on your part. Many of the excellent design possibilities of print are simply not available in ePUBs. What I intend to do is give you a list of changes you must make to get a validated ePUB. The good news is that several things that I would have had to mention for CS5.5 are no longer necessary for CS6.

Digital books are a very different world. You must rethink your concept of a book in order to design one that will work for ePUBs and Kindle books. Let's talk about some of these necessary changes.

Why are ebooks so different?

The most important factor is adjustable type: The reader controls font sizes globally and can override your font choices. At this point, even as a designer you don't get much control over font choice, font style, font size, font spacing, or typography in general. These critical typographic concerns are downgraded to CSS capabilities—but with far fewer fonts even on the iPad. OpenType features are not available. We are back to the very limited 256 character choices.

This is changing as you read this: As I am writing, it is now recommended that you embed fonts for Nook and Kindle. I have worked with the Kindle export and it seems to work well for Fire, but the Mac readers are still stuck with the old capabilities. I can only see the embedded fonts in Amazon's Kindle Previewer. The best I can get out of Amazon is that they are still stripped out by the converter in the Kindle digital Publishing (KDP) uploader. I tried with Nook, but the embedded fonts encrypt the ePUB, and PubIt will not accept it. So, today in June 2012, embedded fonts are still a fond hope.

As a reader, you get a few fonts with up to four styles, a dozen sizes (maybe), and that's it. As a designer, you get the number of fonts available in your ereaders or Apps. This is usually just serif and sans serif, unless you're on an iPad, four typestyles (regular, italic, bold, and bold Italic), largely unlimited sizes & line spacing, alignments, indents, nested styles, a couple of list styles, six headline styles plus unlimited classes, and all of this directly out of InDesign.

The second major factor is the single column layout: Without coding—cracking the ePUB to edit the raw code—there is nothing that can be done about this. There is a real hope that the CSNext version of InDesign will deal with this. InDesign and Dreamweaver in CS5.5 were supposed to be interim versions to prepare the way for the full implementation of HTML5 and CSS3—whatever that means in software capabilities. CS6 made some radical steps forward in this, but Liquid Layout with its automatic column additions and graphic resizing and remasking for various ereaders and smart phones has no real bearing on ePUBs. It's developed for use in app design for magazines with tablets—where multi-column pages are the norm. For now, we are not there with ePUBs unless you are a better than competent coder.

CS6 will now export floating graphics: It is possible to set up graphics in an Anchored Object with an Object style which will float your graphics to the right or left. The margins still cause trouble, and you must do the graphics as a fixed size, so far. But the capability now exists—more on this in a bit.

How much do we change? Everything.

So, it is obvious that we must rethink our book designs. The real question is how much do we want to change in the conversion from print to ebook? The unavoidable answer, at present, is that we need a complete redo. This goes quite a bit beyond simple repurposing. But it is mostly just redefining styles.

Designing for repurposing: This can certainly be done. What it requires is a clear idea of what is going to be needed for the conversion. So what we need to do is talk about what you will need to set up in your print versions. In order to make your ePUB look as good as possible we need to think reasonably about how to set up our documents so they can be converted quickly.

Document size

At present for ePUBs I am using a document with a Digital Publishing intent: iPad vertical (768x1024 pixels), with 84 pixel margins right and left; and 82 pixel margins top and bottom. This gives me a Primary text frame of 600x860 which is the maximum image size for an image in an ePUB on an iPad2. The Retina resolution (double the iPad2) has no standardized techniques, yet. I'll cover Kindle later.

Graphic format, size, and resolution

This one is rough. They always look horrible when compared to print. What you basically need to understand is that you will be using relatively large Web graphics—but 72 dpi not 300 dpi. This is obviously a serious conflict with the way we have been working in print for the past decade. Basically you need 600×860 pixel [iPad2 maximum], RGB JPEGs. The Nook and Fire have different image size requirements as we'll see in a bit.

This obviously takes some planning ahead as you will be using grayscale images (vector PDFs if possible) in your print documents—in most cases. You'll have CMYK images if you print in color. So from the beginning, as you write and create, you need to save RGB versions of your color images.

At this point, even though the ePUB3 spec accepts SVG, which is a vector form of graphic, none of the ereaders do—with the possible exception of Kindle Fire and iBooks2 books produced with Apple's iBooks2 Author. Neither InDesign nor Dreamweaver can deal with SVG images at this point.

Everything in one story

Eliminate all separate stories

> **The problem isn't with the ePUB standard**
>
> The problem is with the software we have available to implement that standard and with the dedicated ereaders available to read what we publish. I am always saddened when I read my ePUBs in Ibis (a browser-based ereader). They look so much better than is possible without coding in Kindle, or Nook. This is a brand new capability. All I have to do is remember how limited PageMaker 4.2 and Quark 3 were when I began in digital publishing in 1991.

Remember that everything in an ePUB must be in one story and inline. This is a radical conversion in many cases. And you will need to do it by hand. The new Articles Panel is supposed to be a help, but in my experience it takes longer to order things in this way and it is certainly not a flawless conversion. So, I drag'n'drop any separate stories into a location that makes sense—rewriting as necessary to keep the copy flowing well. Again, simply repurposing is not a good idea. ePUBs are a very different reading experience and we must adapt to it.

What I find is that concepts which can be easily shown with typography are completely lost in an ePUB. I commonly need to rewrite copy to deal with this fact because much of my writing is about typography. Type in an anchored sidebar usually needs to be rewritten and placed into a different location to make sense as a part of the one story. Many sidebars can be simply eliminated.

For very graphic books like mine with the wrapped graphics, I simply redo the object style for the graphics so that it drops them in inline in their own paragraph with auto leading. Moving graphics around to make the most sense becomes easy with the new drag'n'drop anchoring controls built into the frame edge—upper side, right corner. Simply drag them into position and convert them to inline with a shortcut.

Very limited anchored graphics: convert most to inline

Wrapped graphics are definitely doable, but you'll need to crack the code and edit the XHTML files and the CSS. In CS6, anchored graphics can be set to float right or left, but the margins are messed up. The biggest missing capability is in setting sizing to percentages. Now, all you can do is set the pixel width.

Dealing with captions: It will really help you work on the ePUB code generated by InDesign if you group your captions with your graphics instead of inserting them inline. This is the only way InDesign adds a div automatically at this point, for those of you who know what a div is.

Be patient with all of this. Adding ebooks to the publishing repertoire is a very complex operation for Adobe. InDesign CS6 has laid much of the groundwork for HTML5 and CSS3 plus the beginnings of ePUB3 support and the CSNext version (a year or so from now) will do even better. We have been assured by Adobe that ePUB3 is very high on their priority list. They have a good reputation of bringing these things online—and for doing it better than we expected. I know I certainly did not expect Liquid layout, yet we got that for CS6. It may only apply to magazines, but ePUB3 support is coming—both in InDesign and in ereaders. The iPad reads ePUB3 docs now, in fact.

Fixing the styles

Eventually we are going to edit the exported tags. But for now I want to talk about how the styles need to change. The easiest way is to simply start editing the copy and changing the styles as we get to them. We must bear in mind that sidebars or anchored graphics require hand coding work at this point—unless you convert them to inline text and graphics (which I recommend).

Again, I often find I need to rewrite copy to deal with the reality of the ePUB reading experience. Do not hesitate to do that. Your ePUB will have a different ISBN# anyway, if you get one.

Font changes

Even though the ePUB spec says we can embed fonts, this is still very tricky. My current recommendation is to choose fonts that are available on the iPad. For the Nook and Fire, we can theoretically embed fonts but you must make sure that you are using fonts with the proper licensing. ***No font supplier I know of is dealing with this yet.***

With iOS5 the iPad supports 58 font families

I've not heard of any changes for iOS6 yet. However, out of these 163 fonts 37 of them in 17 families are Hebrew, Indic, Thai, Tibetan, Chinese, Japanese, or Arabic. So, there are really 126 fonts in 41 families which we can use for English and the rest of the European languages. I'm sorry I can't help you with the rest.

Font choices are always a highly personal thing. I'm going to suggest my personal tastes and give you reasons. You make up your own mind. I'm going to just mention the ugly ones you should never use: Courier or New Courier. These eight fonts should never be used unless you are trying to evoke a period or make a historical statement or something strange. **But almost everyone believes they are hideous fonts (not to mention very difficult to read).**

Fonts with compromised reader reactions

Next we have fonts that are not bad designs, but they have issues—some of them fatal. I don't use them.

- Arial + a rounded style: There are five choices here—regular, italic, bold and bold italic plus the Rounded Bold. Arial is the ugly cousin of Helvetica used to avoid the royalties (as far as I know). These fonts plus Times make up the core of some of the most overused fonts in existence. Plus they are the default for bureaucracies.
- Helvetica [6] & Helvetica Neue [11]: Both of these families are available in regular, italic, bold and bold italic, plus many more. There is nothing really wrong with these fonts for heads and subheads. But readability is a real issue. The main problem is the bureaucratic overtones that these fonts share with Arial.
- Times New Roman: This family has regular, italic, bold and bold italic. Though the bold pair tend to be too narrow and ugly with plugged counters, the real problem is the bureaucratic associations.

Bureaucratic fonts: These are the fonts that have been the defaults in Office, Publisher, and similar non-professional page layout tools for decades—Arial, Helvetica, Times, and Times Roman. They are not very pretty fonts. But, the true situation is that non-professionals who use nothing but software defaults are the only people who use these fonts. In fact, most bureaucracies have standardized them and require their use. The result is that they trigger our ***bureaucratic drivel*** filter.

For example, if you watch when you open your mail or when you receive handouts, you will see that bureaucratic output is quickly consigned to the trash—usually without being read. We know that there is no content in these things. Bureaucratic output is produced purely to prove to administrators that something was done—even though we all know that nothing was done except some committee meetings. Our experience tells us these are a waste of time to read.

So also, there are many people (like myself) who simply toss obvious Word output without reading it. Beyond that, default Word and Publisher output is barely readable. The default typography settings are very bad and obvious. There are simply too many really bad associations with these fonts to use them.

Versatile fonts for typography

The iPad gives us several quite good choices here. These are font families that are relatively easy to read and comfortable for the reader. There are several fine serif choices, and a lesser selection of sans serif families. However, there are enough choices for you to be able to make your ePUBs unique, stylish and very readable.

For body copy you need at least regular, bold, and italic versions for your typographic needs. A bold italic is nice—but not often needed. You'll need these fonts installed on your machine to use them in InDesign. If not you'll be forced to add them by hand in the code. These are installed with Lion (OSX.7).

Serif choices for body copy

The copy in brackets and sans serif are the font names as you need to write them in the CSS code. In most cases CS6 will do this correctly for you.

- Baskerville: There are six choices—[Baskerville, Baskerville-Italic, Baskerville-Bold, and Baskerville-BoldItalic, plus Baskerville-SemiBold & Baskerville-SemiBoldItalic]. This is an extremely elegant font, very readable—a little cool and distant. It's a bit formal for my taste now, but it was my first font purchase back in 1991 when I started using PageMaker.

- Bodoni 72: This is the ITC translation of Bodoni's Papale (or Papal) version of his fonts. These fonts are extremely elegant but a bit difficult to use in smaller sizes because of the extreme modulation (contrast in stroke widths). There are seven fonts here, including a true small cap version of book.
  Bodoni 72: [BodoniSvtyITCTT-Book, BodoniSvtyITCTT-BookIta, [BodoniSvtySCITCTT-Book], & BodoniSvtyITCTT-Bold]
  Bodoni 72 Oldstyle: [BodoniSvtyOSITCTT-Book, BodoniSvtyOSITCTT-BookIta, & BodoniSvtyOSITCTT-Bold] The Oldstyle version has lowercase figures which is very nice.
- Cochin: There are four choices—[Cochin, Cochin-Italic, Cochin-Bold, and Cochin-BoldItalic]. This has been my choice recently—largely because of the uniquely splashy italics. I suspect it is a fad on my part, but I like this family.
- Didot: There are three choices—[Didot, Didot-Italic, and Didot-Bold]. This is a more uptight and mechanically crafted Bodoni. I'd call it prickly and scrawny, but then I don't like it.
- Georgia: There are four choices—[Georgia, Georgia-Italic, Georgia-Bold, and Georgia-BoldItalic]. This font has oldstyle figures and is very solid and readable. A Web-safe font family
- Hoefler Text: There are four choices—[HeoflerText, HeoflerText-Italic, HeoflerText-Black, and HeoflerText-BlackItalic]. This font has oldstyle figures and is very solid and readable. It is more traditional in form than Georgia.
- Palatino: There are four choices—[Palatino-Roman, Palatino-Italic, Palatino-Bold, and Palatino-BoldItalic]. This is a very good looking and extremely readable font with a chiseled, calligraphic look. It uses uppercase figures. Its only problem is some overuse because it was one of the original

PostScript fonts when desktop publishing first started. A Web-safe font family

New for iOS5

Baskerville and Cochin have been removed from the iBooks menu on your iPad. But you can still specify these fonts in your CSS. Charter, Iowan, and Seravek have been added, but I can find nothing out about using them in your ePUB style. If it's important to you, try it. But they are not very distinctive fonts. So, I'm not even trying to use them at this point.

Sans serif choices for body copy

- Futura: There are two choices– [Futura-Medium & Futura-MediumItalic]. Futura is barely usable for body copy. This font is a standard in some areas (like here in southern Minnesota). But it is very hard to read, so my recommendation is to use it only for heads—sparingly.
- Futura: [Futura-CondensedMedium & Futura-CondensedExtraBold] You will not be able to choose a bold version with a character style but will have to choose both of these as separate fonts.
- Gill Sans: There are six choices—[GillSans-Light, GillSans-LightItalic, GillSans, GillSans-Italic, GillSans-Bold, and GillSans-BoldItalic]. This is the only iPad sans family with any sense of style. It is also more readable than any other sans offering except Optima [which is nearly a serif design].
- Optima: There are five choices—[Optima-Regular, Optima-Italic, Optima-Bold, and Optima-BoldItalic— plus Optima-ExtraBlack]. This font is one of the most readable sans serifs. There is a little flare at the ends of the strokes. It's been overused in my experience so I no longer use it (but that's just me).
- Trebuchet MS: There are four choices—[TrebuchetMS, TrebuchetMS-Italic, TrebuchetMS-Bold, and TrebuchetMS-BoldItalic]. This is a good-looking easy to read sans that is slightly chunky. A Web-safe font family

- Verdana: There are four choices—[Verdana, Verdana-Italic, Verdana-Bold, and Verdana-BoldItalic]. This is an excellent font for headers. The large x-height makes it a lot larger than the rest of these fonts, but it reads well. A Web-safe font family

Stylish display options

Finally we have a group of fonts that are quite stylized and really only usable for larger headlines. They are usually too hard to read in smaller sizes—or, they have limited style choices. They do make excellent style statements for various demographics. You just need to be careful.

- Academy Engraved LET: [AcademyEngraveLETPlain] Very elegant, almost bankish or financial
- American Typewriter: [AmericanTypewriter-Light, AmericanTypewriter-CondensedLight, AmericanTypewriter, AmericanTypewriter-Condensed, AmericanTypewriter-Bold, AmericanTypewriter-CondensedBold]. The only reason this is here and not in body copy is that there are no italics.
- Bradley Hand: [BradleyHandITCTT-Bold] A slightly uptight script that looks like modern cursive printing—a little.
- Chalkboard SE: [ChalkboardSE-Light, ChalkboardSE-Regular, and ChalkboardSE-Bold]. A handwriting font.
- Chalkduster: [Chalkduster] More loose than Bradley Hand
- Copperplate: [Copperplate-Light, Copperplate, and Copperplate-Bold]. The de facto standard for lawyers and bankers. It only comes with small caps.
- Marion: [Marion-Regular, Marion-Italic, and Marion-Bold]. Described as being like Century Schoolbook, sorta. What this actually means is that it looks a little heavy and has relatively heavy serifs. This one is not installed with Lion.

- Marker Felt: [MarkerFelt-Thin & MarkerFelt-Wide]. A narrow, dark and more structured hand-written script
- Noteworthy: [Noteworthy-Light & Noteworthy-Bold] This is an upright handwriting style reminiscent of Tekton.
- Papyrus: [Papyrus & Papyrus-Condensed]. A raging fashion, but elegant and pretty.
- Party LET: [PartyLetPlain] Sixties junk [in my humble opinion] but then the sixties were why I dropped out [says the old hippy].
- Snell Roundhand: [Snell Roundhand, Snell Roundhand-Bold, & Snell Roundhand-Black] Standard formal script
- Zapfino: Very flashy calligraphy—the sizing is messed up so there are a lot of overlaps from line to line. Use with care. It will take a lot of extra line spacing and/or margins to work well.

Remember! Apple can change these at whim: I've heard rumors of some new fonts for the Retina Display in the new iPad, but I've found nothing so far.

Plus, the reader can change fonts at will: Reflow is the goal. That trumps typography in an ebook. Also remember, that an ePUB on an iPad is the typographic wonder of the ebook world. Even Kindle Fire and Nook now support ePUB and have tablets with slightly better font options—but nothing like the choices built into iOS.

According to an article on ireaderreview.com the following fonts are available on the older ereaders. You quickly see that the iPad and iPhone give us exceptional choices. The Kindle Fire is certainly headed in that direction. It has eight fonts, but I can't find out what they are for sure [probably Droid Sans and Droid Serif]. I don't even know if this is eight font families or eight individual fonts. So things are indeed getting better, but slowly.

- Kindle uses PMN Caecilia a condensed version of Caecilia, and a sans serif option: this is a very readable slab serif but I haven't found out what the sans serif is.

- Nook uses Helvetica Neue (sans-serif), Amasis (serif), and Light Classic (serif): Amasis is a more humanist slab serif.
- Sony uses Dutch 801 and Swiss 701: A Times variant and a Helvetica variant.
- Android OS has three font families: Droid Sans, Droid Sans Mono and Droid Serif and this includes the Nook Tablet and Kindle Fire.

The Kindle, Nook, and Sony choices may be easily readable on their devices. But they certainly do not provide good typographic choices for a designer.

Your only real font choices [outside the iPad & iPhone] are serif or sans, plus you can add italic and bold: The problem, of course, is that serif or sans were not a font choice in InDesign 5.5 or earlier. The good news is that InDesign CS6 now adds those choices automatically when you export to ePUB.

Embedded fonts: iPad, Nook and Kindle Fire all take embedded fonts now, but licenses which cover ePUB use are virtually non-existent at this point. It will come though. The uploaders can't handle them though.

However, we must remember that ebooks using the currently limited choices are selling like crazy. Kindle has a huge majority of the overall market. If you want to sell to that market, you need to make a book that fits their paradigm. In my case, non-fiction about InDesign and font design sell about equally on iBooks and Kindle (plus print is still about a third of sales).

Size & Leading changes

We have quite a bit of control here. In an ePUB the font sizing and spacing must be specified in ems or pixels. InDesign is doing it in ems in CS6. Basically, 12 point type is converted to one em. Leading is converted to a multiple of that em. On the iPad's high resolution screen, one em is actually 16 pixels high (I guess that's 32 pixels for the Retina). [But the reader can change it all by whim—though the size proportions will remain.]

Small Caps & All CAPS now work

Of course, the fonts used do not have true small caps, in most cases. So, any typographically excellent true small caps would have to be in fonts that have them like Copperplate & Bodoni 72 Small Caps.

No special fonts: convert to graphic

At this point if you need a special font, you need to make it into a graphic. Sometimes selecting the words and choosing Create Outlines will do it. But the resulting rasterized graphic will likely be a bad size and very pixilated. Normally, it is necessary to make a separate PDF graphic with that type to rasterize into Photoshop. Then save as a Web graphic and place into your ePUB document. You will be doing this a lot—at least until ebook readers & distributors accept SVG vector files.

Embedding fonts has many legal issues: You need to be careful which fonts you use. Though you can embed any font you have on your computer—there are two major problems. First, it is not likely that any font you have has been hinted for 72 dpi use. Second, none of the major distribution sites like MyFonts have decided on an ePub license. So, if there is any doubt (and believe me there is), do not embed fonts unless you are sure you own the rights and that it will look good.

Remove all indents, left and right: from lists

Lists are much better in CS6. In 5.5, all you can do is delete all special indents you set up. Make it a numbered or bulleted list (with no special bullet) and let InDesign do the translation. Not good, but anything else requires you to crack the code and set up special CSS rules for the ol and ul tags. You can now make li classes in the export tags dialog to control fonts and such in CS6. CS5.5 ignores all of this. [Waiting for CSNext]

Eliminate fancy bullets: from lists

You must crack the ePUB and change the CSS to use special bullets—either from CSS choices or graphics.

Add chapter breaks before a section gets over 300K

Supposedly graphics are not counted here. But long files with no chapter breaks will not work. You must set up a H1 style in export tags (usually your headline) and specify it as the chapter break.

Eliminate all soft returns.

You must crack the ePUB and change the HTML to add the soft returns. You will get rid of all of them when exporting the ePUB.. **But understand,** soft returns are a real problem when the reader can change fonts and font sizes at will while he or she is reading.

Eliminate all OpenType feature use

Nothing can be done about this. Current ebook readers do not support OpenType features—yet. However, they will. It is part of the HTML5/CSS3 scenario and therefore usable in the ePUB standard eventually.

Eliminate tabs & tables: or rework the code

Put your tabular materials in a separate InDesign file and export it as a PDF to rasterize and place into your ePUB document. The resulting pixilated type is the same problem we have been dealing with throughout this exercise. HTML/CSS does not support tabs so you'll need to do tables in the code.

A table is a set of zero leading returns to add a new text frame with a specified offset. InDesign 5.5 will export the tables, but they will look bad with all borders and backgrounds deleted or changed. CS6 does better and HTML/CSS can do good tables, but InDesign isn't excellent yet. You will probably want to edit the code or set up an InDesign doc for the table, make a PDF, and rasterize it in Photoshop 600 pixels wide.

InDesign CS6 has improved table export quite a bit: I have not worked much with this so far, but here is the official Adobe word on this feature. They have added support for converting InDesign's table cell styles to CSS in the exported EPUB. The EPUB table dimensions now include attributes for column width and row minimum height. I'll blog about this once I get time to try it. So far, simple tables seem to work well

Eliminate paragraph rules

HTML/CSS does not support rules though you do have border controls. InDesign drops any rules upon export at this time. The only rules you have available are Underline and Strikethrough without any customizing.

If you need the rules, you can create graphics that you can place before and/or after your paragraphs. The only problem with that is the lack of spacing control. Plus there is no way to do an overlap so you cannot have a rule as a bar from which the type reverses out to white. For that you need to edit the code and set the background, alignment, and padding for the paragraph

Eliminate borders

You can only use borders on a graphic. The ePUB readers cannot put borders on a frame. For CS5.5, to add a border to a paragraph or group of paragraphs you need to edit the HTML and often add a div in the code. For CS6, you can add a stroke, fill, and corner options to your frames holding your graphics. InDesign still rasterizes them into graphics, but at least the look is there.

Graphic frames with live type: This should be easily possible with CSS, but InDesign does not support this well enough to use at this point.

CS5.5 & better now work with nested styles

Prior to 5.5, we had to hand format any character styles by selecting the type and applying the style. Now you can use nested styles. In the exported ePUB they are converted to spans which you can control with the Export Tags dialog. Of course, you need to do all the changes to make those character styles work in an ePUB.

Making these changes & proofing

What needs to be done now is to go through all the styles used in your print document and convert them to work within ePUB limitations. Then export your ePUB and open it in Adobe Digital Editions–Adobe's free ePUB reader and Ibis–Safari Books Online's online browser reader. Ibis shows many things that ADE doesn't. Calibre works also. But none of these options compares with what you will actually see in the ereader. You can set the export options to automatically open your ePUB after it is exported.

> **If you own an iPad, Nook, and/or Kindle [Fire]:** open the ePUB in it to see how it will look there. Make sure you import a copy of the ePUB into your iPad. It is especially important to check out the graphics and see how they fit. Adjust spacing as well as you possibly can.

If you are typographically trained and visually sensitive, this first attempt at an ePUB will be a horrible shock: The typographic ugliness of HTML after you have so carefully crafted your typography is a major hit to the senses. No kerning, tracking, or careful spacing. All the controls are very crude—displayed on a low resolution screen.

Take a deep breath!

Now get on with it: You've learned to deal with the low quality as far as Websites are concerned. [If you haven't—shame on you!] This is the reality of ePUB. Now your goal is to make it as easy to read as possible. Make the window narrow enough to be readable and go to it. It is likely that your first attempts will require you to fix several of your styles. Thankfully, they control the entire document globally because everything is formatted with no local formatting (if you've followed my instructions in *Writing In InDesign Second Edition*). This is yet another reason why the use of styles is so critical.

Deal with reality

Do not hang on to impossible requirements. The more simple you make your typography, the better it will work in this greatly restricted environment. There is nothing wrong with ePUB and the ePUB standard. It is simply different and requires a new sense of design. As

InDesign improves we will have more control. For now we just do the best we can do.

ePUB does give us much more

If we quit looking at ePUBs from the background of the printed book and start looking from the background of ebooks, then we can see how much we have available in an ePUB—especially in iBooks2 and Ibis. Just focus on readability. If your readers have to work at reading your book, they'll try changing the size—but more likely they'll just quit reading.

Setting the TOC (THIS IS REQUIRED)

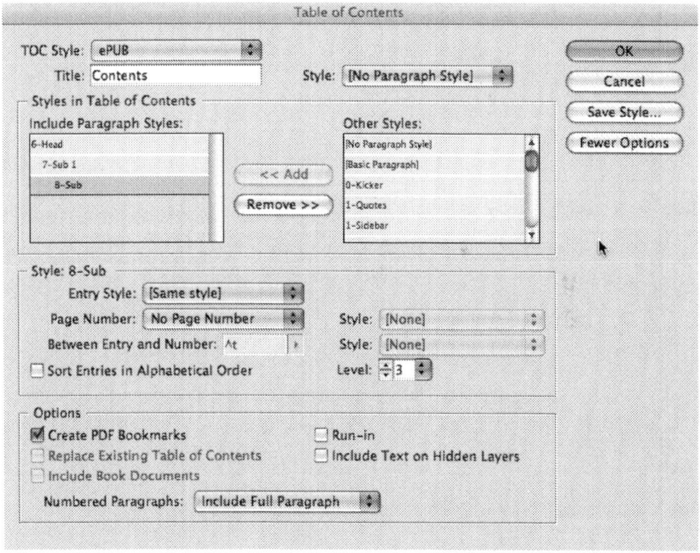

You do need to set up a TOC (Layout>> Table of Contents). You will chose this Table of Contents style in the ePUB Export dialog. The styles you choose for your TOC will be added to the bookmarks in the column to the left of your ePUB. You do not do leaders or page numbers as leaders do not work and page numbers do not exist in ebooks [more accurately said: the page numbers change all time as the reader changes fonts and/ or type size].

The only changes I have made are to make the TOC much more simple. The complex Contents lists become a huge hand full at the beginning of an ebook. What you probably want is a simple listing of the chapter heads.

Adding page breaks with your chapter heads

This is a very important part of setting up your styles. ePUBs do not support page breaks—with one exception. If you have a style set up as a headline, with the keeps set up to start on the next page, the ePUB will start a new chapter when you use that paragraph style. But you must choose it when you export the ePUB. You find this choice in the ePUB Export Options dialog box: Break Document at Paragraph Style with a popup menu to pick the style.

Practicality rules in these things. You can spend time and money trying to figure out why these things are so or you can publish books.

I publish.

Writing the metadata (THIS IS REQUIRED)

You need to write the metadata before you export the ePUB. In the capture on the next page, this is just partially completed. The important things here are the title, description, and keywords. The keywords and the use of those keywords in your book title is very important. This is how your readers find your book online. You need to take this very seriously. You will get better with these things as you gain experience in self-publishing.

Hopefully, you worked all this out when you released your book for print. You find this metadata dialog in the File menu under the File Info command. It is required to fill out this description page. It contains the information primarily used by the search engine spiders. That should say enough about its importance.

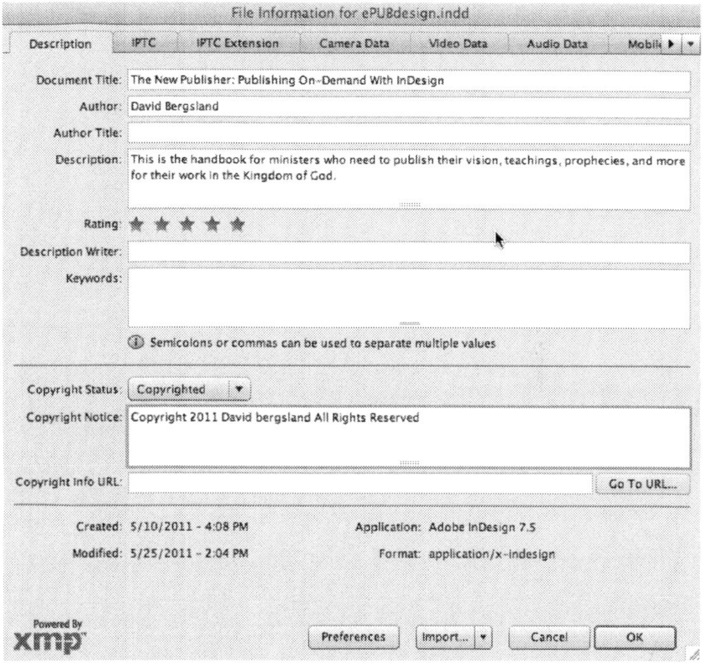

There are some new strict rules

These rules are Apple's rules, as far as I can tell. However, some of them may be Lulu paranoia. It doesn't matter. Do what they ask. You do want to sell your ePUBs, right? They include things like the metadata title must be identical to the copy found on the cover. It must be in title case except for a half dozen or so tiny words. There are several others things like this.

Here are just a few from Lulu's page, but they change all the time as the acceptance of standards increases. Lulu currently accepts ePUB2:

- Title must match everywhere: metadata, cover, and book's title page
- No advertisements or links.

- No mention of included materials that don't exist in the digital product (Example: CD, poster, etc.).
- Cannot up-sell to a version of the product that is more complete.
- Do not use character which require entity references in the description (Example: &, -, or –, etc.)
- Do not use font sizes in the description (Example: <font face="Helvetica" size="3">)
- Cannot mislead buyers or misrepresent the ebook (Example: An illustrated guide containing no illustrations or pictures).
- Subtitles are particularly important for differentiating multiple books in a series that share the same title.
- Improperly formatted HTML tags in the description can cause a garbled description in retail channels.
- Titles and Subtitles incorrectly capitalized. The first letter of all words in the title and subtitle should be capitalized, except for the following words: a, an, and, for, from, of, or, the, to. The first and last word of the title and subtitle should always be capitalized.
- Use of HTML lists in description
- Titles beginning with articles should display properly. EX: A Tale of Two Cities, not Tale of Two Cities, A
- Must have a valid description. Ex: Do not use the title.
- Multiple blank pages. Especially at the beginning of the book. Please remember to remove blank pages before converting to ePUB

There are many more like this on the *eBook Retail Distribution Guidelines* page of the Lulu site. If you do not follow all of them precisely, they will not publish your book.

Setting the Export Tags

New to InDesign CS5.5: As mentioned, this new ability to open a single dialog box and set all the HTML tags and add the CSS classes for each style is huge. It is a real disappointment that we cannot edit these class rules, but it makes it much easier to edit the CSS. CS6 is good enough for me, now. I quit cracking the ePUB to edit.

Forcing InDesign to write usable CSS

Sometimes I feel so stupid. The solution to the incomplete CSS in exported ePUBs for 5.5 and 6 is so much more simple than I thought. Your mind just seems to turn a little corner and the solution pops up.

My beef with InDesign CS5.5's ePUBs was the need to edit the CSS. I posted several times on my blog and published a couple free booklets about fixing the ePUB CSS. What I wrote was accurate. It's not difficult, as long as you know HTML and CSS and can work in Dreamweaver to fix this stuff. But my frustration is that I don't think you should be forced into DW to make an ePUB. It turns out that what I wrote simply is not necessary in most cases.

You can easily force InDesign to write good CSS

Well, that's a bit of an overstatement. The Web developer purists will be shrieking. But, you can easily make InDesign write CSS that controls all of your type in the ePUB. The problem is that InDesign does not define the basic tags: h1-6, p, ol, ul, and so on. It probably does better in CS6, but I still use the tag.class naming procedure described below.

What I suggested before [in CS5.5] is that you map your tags so that all you need to do is open the CSS in Dreamweaver and add definitions for all the basic tags you need. That still works. And in many ways that is still the way to go for reasons we'll mention in a bit.

However, you can easily force InDesign to write CSS rules that will control all of your type without the need to edit the CSS afterward. What you need to do is make sure that you specify a class for all your styles as well as a tag. Let's take a look at what I just exported for the ePUB for Writing in InDesign. I opened the Edit All Export Tags... dialog and set up the tags and classes.

Style	Tag	Class
[No Paragraph Style]	p	none
¶ [Basic Paragraph]	p	basic
¶ 0-Kicker	h5	kicker
¶ 1-Quotes	p	quote
¶ 1-SidebarBody	p	sidebar
¶ 2-body	p	standard
¶ 2-Description	p	indented
¶ 2-No first	p	nofirst
¶ 2-run-in	p	nested
¶ 3-bullet-tabbed	li	tabbed
¶ 3-Bulleted	li	sans
¶ 3-Numbered	li	serif
¶ 4-BoldSideHead	h4	side
¶ 5-Tips	p	nestedindent
¶ 6-Head	h1	chapter
¶ 7-Sub 1	h2	normal
¶ 8-9(WavyRule)	h3	italic
¶ 8-Sub	h3	normal
¶ TripleNested	p	triple
A Blue	strong	blue
A 1-bodyBOLD	strong	serif
A 1-Head Bold	strong	bold
A 2-Italic	em	italic
A 3-ListRegular	strong	regular
A 3-Version	strong	small
A Page#	em	small
A Red	strong	red

Notice I added tags for all the styles. For the lists I was using li plus classes, but this is still dropped upon export in CS6. InDesign adds the ul and ol tags for CSS lists, but we have no way to edit them in InDesign. You need to leave them as [Automatic] for now.

The same is true with all the tags for tables (though CS6 captures Cell Style data). If I want any fancy sidebar rules with backgrounds and reversed type and all of that, I'll still need to edit the CSS.

But this will work, and it will look remarkably close to what I see in InDesign. I'm waiting for CSNext to get more control. I'm tired of editing the CSS in Dreamweaver—so I quit, as mentioned.

What changed are the basic tags

I used to make my heading h1 with no class. Now I have added a class of chapter. I used to make my first level of subhead (Style 7-Sub 1) h2, now I add a class of normal. Even my basic paragraph tag (Style: 2-Body) is now given a class of standard (or normal).

Why add the classes?

That's simple. InDesign will not define p, my basic paragraph tag. But it will define p.normal. It will not define h2, but it will define h2.normal. Is the result wonderfully sleek and elegant XHTML code? No. But it works and all of your typography is controlled. If you do not do this, you are forced to crack the ePUB, open template.css and add the basic tags.

So, the choice is yours. You can now design your ePUB edition of your book in InDesign and directly upload the resultant ePUB with no modifications. The results will look very good.

It is never quite that easy: bad fonts

The problem is that during the massive conversion from your print version to your ePUB version it is extremely likely that you have many styles or locally formatted type that use fonts you cannot use in an ePUB. I was looking at the CSS for the first proof of the ePUB and at the bottom I found many spans asking for fonts I was certain I was not using.

Here we see the Find Font dialog box (Type>> Find Font...) for the InDesign file I used for one of my font design ePUBs. As you can see, the top listings (there were actually sixteen of them) are fonts I didn't want to use in my ePUB, *because* almost every ereader would substitute them out into its defaults. Obviously this is real problem with an ereader like the Nook which only has three fonts available. More importantly, you must be sure it is legal for you to use them. None of these sixteen fonts are available on any ereader unless I am using a browser-based ereader (like Ibis) on my own computer where these fonts are installed.

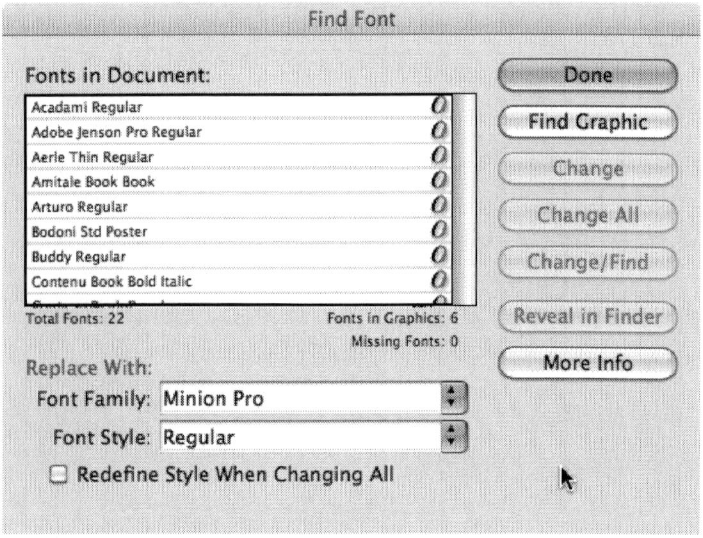

For this ePUB there were about ten of these errant fonts. I carefully decided what to do with each one of those instances. If I click the More Info button you can see above in the Find Font dialog, it will show me the page location of the font use. Once I locate the font flagged in the actual copy of the book, I find I have three choices:

- It may be in a paragraph or character style that was never redefined: In that case I can redefine the style and eliminate the font usage very easily.

- It may be in a graphic: In this case it is usually large enough to convert to outlines and then make a rasterized version of the graphic.
- It may be part of the copy: This will probably not happen to you unless you are like me and write about typography and fonts. In this case, I can select the type and Create Outlines—leaving the outlines type inline in the copy. That will work, but InDesign will convert that outlined type into a coarse bitmap that looks pretty chewed up. Your best choice (for quality) is to rasterize that type in Photoshop and save it as a high quality JPEG at 300 dpi. You can then place that high resolution bitmap graphic inline in your copy and it will look as good as possible.

Many of these things will be solved in CSNext or CSNext+1. But for now, this is what you need to do. Once you have your fonts cleaned up and your export tags set, you can export your ePUB. Type Command+E and select ePUB for your format.

The ePUB export box

With InDesign 5.5, the ePUB export dialog gives us a lot of tools and options as we fight to control our output. There are three pages and many things you need to set. CS6 ramps it up even higher with the choices for EPUB 2.0.1, EPUB 3.0, and EPUB 3.0 with Layout.

At this point, only ePUB 2 works because that is all the distributors are accepting. This will change though. EPUB 3.0 with Layout uses all the possibilities of Liquid Layout and the other new HTML5/CSS3 capabilities added in CS6. No one can read this yet except for a vaporware Adobe Reader which is not available yet.

I am including captures which are set up the way that is working for me currently. This entire area is changing by the week, so any updates will be mentioned in my blogs.

The general page

Let's go through these in order

This page has all changed radically in CS6. Things are moved. New options are available. Adobe is working hard to keep current with a field that is changing so rapidly. Keep light on your feet!

Version: EPUB 2.0.1: This is still the standard and nothing else is accepted by Lulu or Nook. This will change.

Setup

Cover: The choices are None, Rasterize First Page and Choose Image. Once you choose an image that changes to From File as you see above. I design a specific front cover to be used and link it here. That way I can set it up in vector with live type and so on. Just remember to use a JPEG for the cover, at this point. I also place a copy of the cover on page one of the book so it shows up as the first page in the ePUB.TOC Style: You need to choose the one you have set up for your ePUBs. As you can see I call mine ePUB.

Book margin: I set this at 5 pixels, but no one actually seems to use this setting [so leaving it at 0 is probably all right]. I've heard that Nook requires specific settings, but I've heard no complaints about the ePUBs I give them and they are still a small part of my market. I'll change if they ask me to.

Content Order: I use based on page layout. I can do this because I completely re-layout the ePUB version in a new document. Also I do not write XML. I find the articles panel does not give me the control I want. I always place my graphics, for example, in specific locations to read as part of the copy. I do the same with the converted sidebars and all the rest. If your book is simple, you may not need to do this. You'll need to experiment and carefully proof the resulting ePUB to see if the other options work best for you.

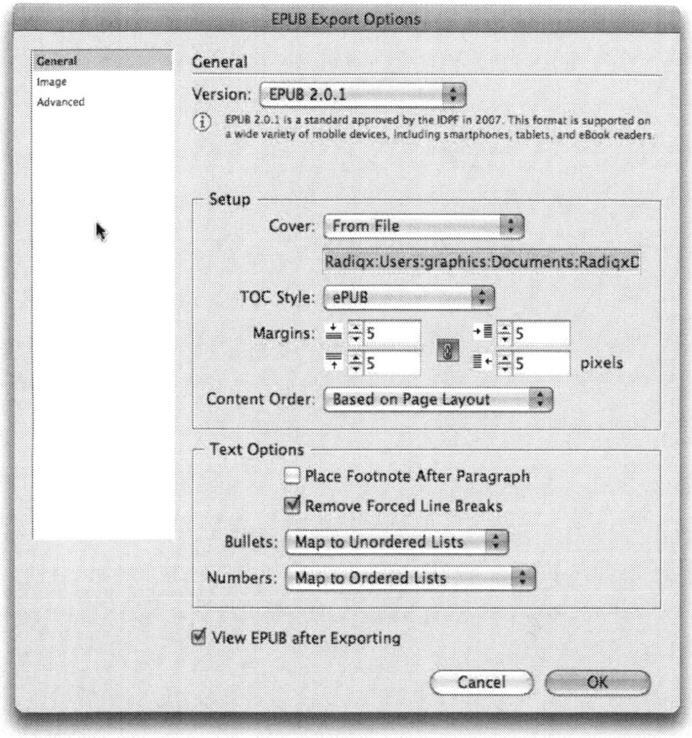

Text Options:

Remove Forced Line Breaks: That's what they are calling soft returns. You must remove them because the type re-wraps horribly when the readers change the size and font (and they will). When InDesign CS6 removes these soft returns it replaces them with a space. That is almost always what you want. But check and make sure.

Bullets & Numbers: Leave them at the defaults [letting InDesign do the mapping]. This is the choice which InDesign uses to add the ul and ol tags. As mentioned, you really need to eliminate all special indents and tabs and let the defaults carry the day. Other than that, you will need to crack the ePUB and edit the CSS file.

View after Exporting: Always check this. Always look over the exported ePUB in ADE or Calibre before you validate and upload. You also need to check in iBooks. Increasingly, I check it out in Ibis, the browser-based ereader from Safari Books Online. It seems to show me the best I can hope for until we get better ereaders. I am still regularly surprised by something that needs to be fixed.

This is not a smooth process yet. It is really good that InDesign can now export ePUBs that can be validated. But it is not smooth yet—and probably not be uneventful until InDesign 9 or 10. But then that is still true for the print versions also and I've been doing that for decades.

The image page

There are no real changes here from 5.5. Again, 5.5 was a large improvement about these things. But there is really no direct guidance. I will share what I know from experience. You may well find new information available by the time you buy this book. I will keep this info updated whenever I hear of new data. Please share it with us if you hear anything.

Finding out information on images is like trying to pull hens' teeth (and no, they don't have teeth). No one seems to want to admit how bad the images really are. The best I can find is that the iPad and most smart phones require 600x800 pixels or less.

The iPad maximum is 600x860 pixels. Nook's maximum size is 600x730 pixels. For Fire it is 600x800. At this point, I make my images to size, and JPEG [in most cases]. I make them wide enough to fit the column of type and place them as inline graphics (unanchored). I do this to get as much help as I can with image sharpness. For photos, you can make them smaller and have them work OK. But, if you need detail make them as large as possible, and that is 600 wide portrait, and 800 wide landscape. The InDesign automated conversion processes trash the graphics. So, I open them in Photoshop and use Save For Web... to save them as JPEGs. I place them at 100% and trust the ereaders to do the best they can.

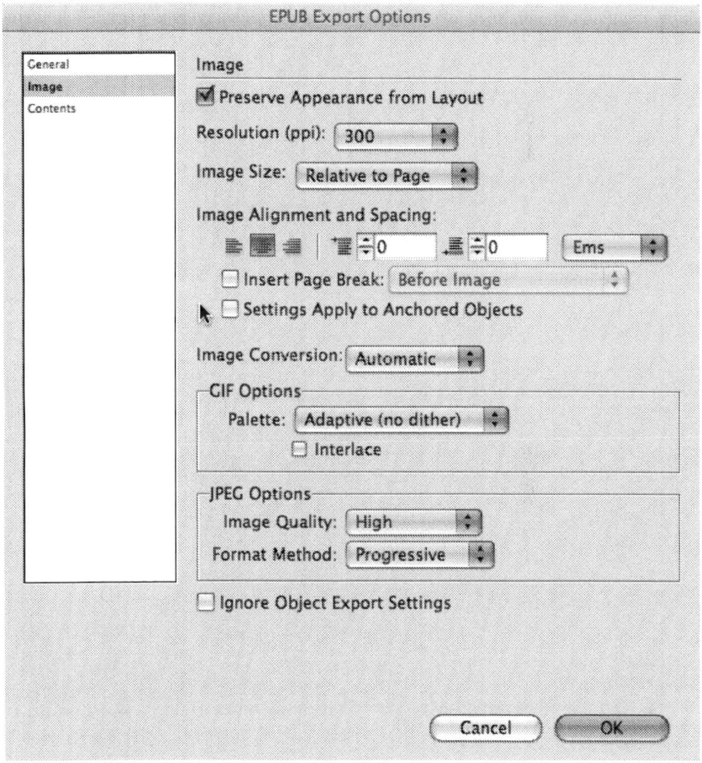

For print, I use PSDs (Photoshop's native format) at 300 dpi. I keep the original PSDs in case I want to go back to the way the image was before the JPEG compression. Then I save JPEG versions at 600 pixels wide to use in the ePUB. This doubles for iPad with Retina (if you can afford the larger file sizes).

Preserve Appearance from Layout: I check this but I am not sure why. It seems to help certain images in iBooks. However, I am continuing to experiment with it. I'll post new knowledge in The Skilled Workman. You need to experiment also.

Remember, ebook graphics are ghastly: I continue to fight the good fight, but you really need to question why you are even including graphics. The iPad does a good job, but the ePUB format itself does not support graphic excellence. The eventual support of SVG (vector) graphics should help solve these problems. But that's only available in iBook Author, at this point. Of course there is now the hope that the high resolution of the new iPad will really help.

Resolution (ppi): 300—you need the highest resolution possible to look good on the better machines like the Retina Displays of the iPad and the iPhones. I imagine the other tablets won't be quite as good, but they will be getting better. If the file size gets too large, I cut it to 150 ppi. We just do the best we can.

Image size: The choices are Fixed and Relative to Page. I now use Relative to Page, and this seems to make good graphics that are the width of the page. I want them the width of the page because they are basically low-res bitmap images. I want them as large as possible to be readable. I haven't had time to thoroughly deal with the Retina specs. But if I have room in the file size, I'll be using graphics at 1200 pixels wides placed at 50%.

Image Alignment and Spacing: Because my images are all inline the alignment is controlled by the paragraph style used and that is flush left, so I don't expect any changes when I click the Left button here. It doesn't make any difference as I make all my images the width of the column. I leave the spacing at the defaults and use auto leading for the special paragraph style I set up to hold my images.

Insert page break: Before Image, After Image, or Both Before and After Image. I've never used it, but I can see its utility.

Image Conversion: I leave this at automatic, and set the JPEG options to High. The image quality in ePUBs is bad enough without any JPEG artifacts produced by compressing the JPEGs too far. However, for my font design book (with nearly 300 graphics) this made my ePUB nearly 20 MB. So, I changed the quality to medium and set the resolution at 150 dpi. Because the images are almost all screen captures, the new ePUB looks very good on the iPad. You must do what you need to do to get the best images possible.

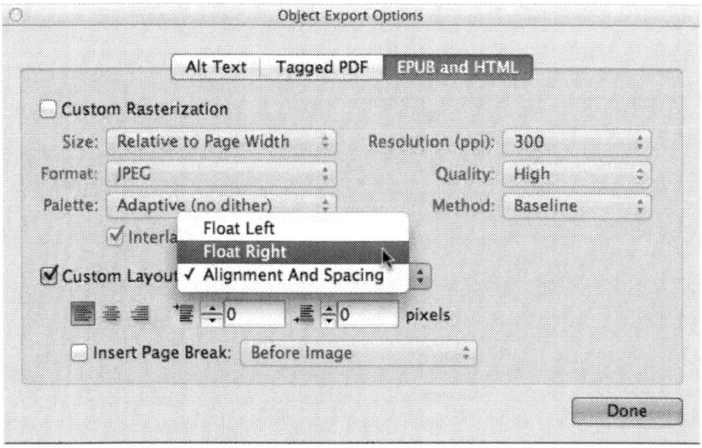

Ignore Object Export Settings: I leave it unchecked because I do not set custom settings for any image—yet. The problem is that Object Export Settings are needed to control anchored objects as sidebars. This is where you add a float to an object to make it align on the left or right margin of your ePUB. The problem is that the controls are still rudimentary in CS6. Plus, you usually need a full-sized graphic to get enough pixels to make it readable.

These will be the controls for anchored text frames used as sidebars. But they are not quite ready for prime time yet. You still have to crack the ePUB and edit the CSS.

Advanced page

This last page is very important and it's changed radically from 5.5. It used to be called Contents.

Split Document: You need to pick your headline style or whatever style you use to start your chapters on a new odd page. This is working well.

EPUB Metadata

Check Include Metadata: For Publisher:, use your company name. Let InDesign generate the Unique ID.

CSS Options

Check Include Style Definitions: This will write the styles you are using into CSS.

Make sure you uncheck "Preserve Local Overrides" and "Include Embedded Fonts": The local overrides will greatly complicate your code. It will add a lot of spans. That said I may start using this as I go ahead. Only Nook and Fire support embedded fonts—yet (and there are bad licensing issues). However, as embedded fonts are the only hope for Android machines, they are coming quickly.

Additional CSS: This requires coding. It may be the best solution but I haven't done much with it yet. But as you'll see in Appendix F, I was working on it hard. My hope was to have a sample CSS file you can use with the sample styles I have you set upon the Website. I'm not making any promises because I really dislike Coding. If InDesign gets good enough I want to be able to simply export and end up with usable ePUBs. At this point, it is close enough so I am no longer worrying about this.

If you link to a CSS file, I would uncheck the "Include Style Definitions" option. You wouldn't want to confuse the poor program.

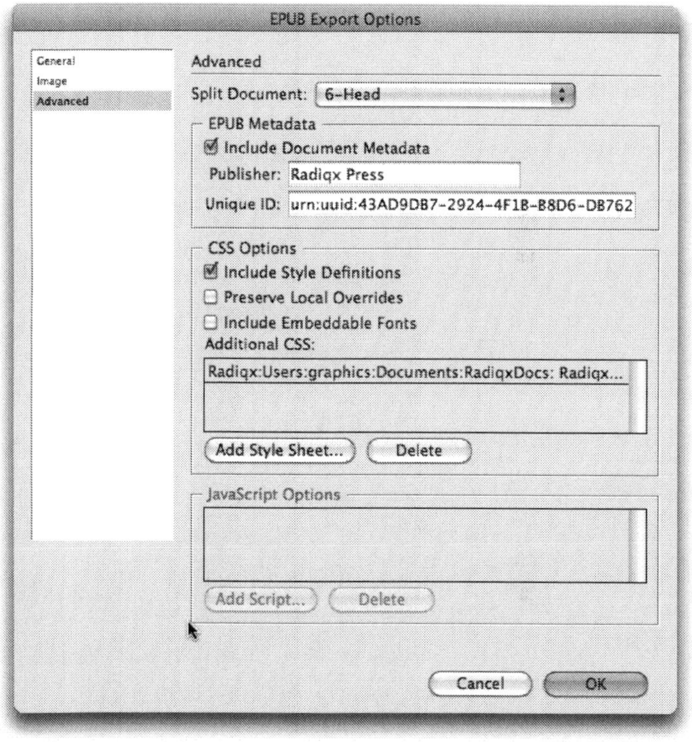

Click OK and you've got an ePUB

It will open in ADE, Calibre, (or your reader of choice). Proof it carefully. Redo as necessary. By now you'll have a good idea what is translating well.

Edit the CSS if you can (or don't if you can't)

The problem is that even with CS5.5 the resulting CSS has some major issues. With CS6 things are much better. Of course, you must know CSS to do anything about it. But some of the things are relatively easy.

- Make sure the font choices are good: I would double-check to at least make sure that the serif and sans serif names are correct. Then make them work for the fonts in the iPad list.
- Define the basic HTML tags: InDesign does not do this in CS5.5. It defines all the classes you set up in the Export Tags dialog, but the basic tags are not defined (unless you force it to with classes as I mentioned earlier).
- Do anything else you can figure out from Castro's *ePUB Straight to the Point*: It all depends on how comfortable you are with code, HTML, and CSS. You can open the whole folder as a site in Dreamweaver. Edit carefully, and work on a copy if you are not good with the code.

Validate it

Redo the proof as often as necessary. When you have what you like, go to: http://validator.idpf.org/

It should validate. The only real problem is that Lulu is still using ePUB Check 1.2 and the validator site is using the beta of version 3. I finally gave up and found an older version of ePUB Check 1.2 (googled it). But both Lulu and validator.idpf.org are getting much better about this and increasingly they let you know what is causing the problem in a manner you can understand (this was not true a year ago).

Upload to Lulu

If it does validate, then you can start a new ebook project at Lulu. As I've mentioned they are an official aggregator for iBookstore. They will give you an ISBN# and get your ePUB listed on iBookstore.

Upload to PubIt!

You can use the same ePUB you produced for Lulu. But now I recommend a new version. I'm going to try embedded fonts as soon as I can find a way to do it. At present PubIt will not accept an ePUB with embedded fonts. YUou need to encrypt the fonts to keep the font designers happy. InDesign does this, but the resulting ePUB is encrypted and PubIt will not accept encrypted ePUBs. At the least, you should check your graphics to make sure that none are taller than 730 pixels. You cannot use Lulu's ISBN (but PubIt does not require one). You'll need a cover with a different resolution.

Converting to Kindle

Until very recently, I gave some very explicit instructions for the construction of the HTML and CSS needed to step back in time to Amazon's MOBI format. It was extremely limited in what was allowed.

Designers are rarely good coders, and writers even less so. InDesign is the best tool we have at present, but there's still a long way to go until some of the typographic niceties we rely on in print are actually available in an ePUB without a lot of hand-coding.

I used Calibre to convert my ePUBs

But this was before I could embed fonts. Now I'm using the Amazon InDesign plug-in for CS5.5 [at the time of this release the new plug-in for CS6 has not been released. If you do not embed fonts, you simply add your ePUB to Calibre and use it to convert your ePUB to MOBI. Google Calibre. It's a free app (shareware, actually).

This week I am experimenting with embedding my own fonts. If you embed fonts, you cannot use Calibre to convert your ePUB. It is locked (to protect the fonts from theft) and Calibre thinks it has DRM. So this book's Kindle version used the plug-in for CS5.5.

As of this weekend in mid-June 2012, Amazon was bouncing ePUBs converted to MOBI with Calibre: There are evidently some issues with Calibre's ability to make KF8 mobi files. I suspect that Calibre will get that fixed soon.

For the Amazon InDesign plug-in

You need to start by doing all the conversions we talked about for building an ePUB. The KF8 format is a

Kindle/Amazon proprietary product, and therefore, it is not Adobe's responsibility to build around it. It is entirely Amazon's responsibility to provide any necessary plug-ins to work with InDesign (which they have done but the CS6 plug-in is not released yet, June 2012).

The Kindle plug-in for InDesign works well for what it does, but it is only useful if you are using ID to build a document with the single purpose of exporting that file to MOBI for use on the Kindle (Legacy e-ink and Fire). You can use the document you created for ePUB export to start with.

- The plugin only recognizes the most basic of text formatting and anchored images: (but we've already covered that with ePUB design).
- It cannot handle nested styles: so all run-in heads will need to be formatted by hand.
- It does do a good job of creating working hyperlinks: based on properly built cross-refs, hyperlinks, ID-generated TOC, and footnotes.
- It does do a good job of embedding fonts: Of course, this assumes that you have fonts with a license which allows you to embed them in an ebook.

  As of this weekend in mid-June 2012, the uploader at KDP is still stripping out the fonts: There is no reason that I know of for this, but it si what it is. I'll post on The Skilled Workman when I find out new procedures.

- The plug-in will add eBook section breaks based on separate InDesign files only: It does not recognize InDesign's ability to add breaks via Paragraph style. This is a big problem for those of us doing larger graphically intensive books. We'll need to break our ePUB file in pieces and use the Book panel again.

- The plug-in will also only recognize content order based on the old-school way of ordering: single text thread with inline images. It does not recognize the use of the Articles Panel.

Bottom line for kindle plug-in use:

- The Kindle plug-in for InDesign is ONLY useful if your document/project is redisigned and intended for Kindle only: For that purpose, it works well.

I still recommend Calibre conversions unless you are trying to embed fonts for the Kindle Fire

You need to download a copy of the Kindle Previewer from Amazon to see the fonts (unless you own a Fire). The Kindle apps for OSX and iOS5 do not show the embedded fonts. So, it's still iffy. But Amazon has promised this will be fixed in the near future.

Subscribe to my blogs, The Skilled Workman or Font Design & Typography On-Demand. I'll keep you up to date on these blogs as new things develop. The Skilled Workman is my main blog. I keep the other one only to supply the subscribers there.

Index

5575082R00033

Printed in Great Britain
by Amazon.co.uk, Ltd.,
Marston Gate.